Members'
Guide to
Marketing

Members'
Guide to
Marketing

J A C K   P I G D E N

GUILD OF MASTER CRAFTSMAN PUBLICATIONS LTD

First published 1992 by
Guild of Master Craftsman Publications Ltd,
166 High Street, Lewes,
East Sussex BN7 1XU

© Guild of Master Craftsman Publications Ltd 1992

ISBN 0 946819 34 3

Designed by Ian Hunt Design

Printed by Grosvenor Press (Portsmouth) Limited

Contents

Introduction

> In the beginning there was an idea - enthusiasm gave it birth, finance gave it life. Eventually it became a product, something everyone would want. Or so everyone thought!
>
> After a time the company failed and the product died with it. Everyone agreed that it was a great idea - it just wasn't exactly what they wanted. Perhaps if it had been available in a different size or colour, maybe just a little bit cheaper...

Such is the cycle of business for many companies. It wasn't that there was anything wrong with the idea - it just wasn't marketed properly. And what is meant by marketing is the subject of this book.

What follows is a marketing guide for all businesses, large and small. At one level it is an introductory course for those unfamiliar with marketing concepts. At another it is a reminder for those employed in marketing of the disciplines necessary for successful implementation of a marketing plan.

At both levels, this book is a route map with clear signposts pointing the way to the preparation of a detailed marketing plan; a plan for the future, to help the business survive and prosper.

There is no one right way to read this book. Some readers will want to start at the beginning and work their way through. For this purpose the sequence of chapters attempts to follow a logical structure. Others will want to read specific sections on advertising, public relations or whatever, and for this purpose each chapter is entire in itself and not overly cross-referenced.

Many readers are exceptionally busy men who do not have a lot of time to spend reading books. For them there is a summary at the end of each chapter. They might find it advisable to skim through the whole book in this way, making notes to refer back to the contents of the chapters that interest them and which could prove useful.

For anyone at any level who has an interest in marketing, or feels that he or she would like to know more about it, it is hoped that this book will be helpful and informative.

1 What Marketing Means

A number of definitions of marketing exist, but most of them are variations on a single theme. In short, marketing is the profitable satisfaction of a customer need.

The whole marketing process begins with a customer need. And any company which identifies a need, is able to satisfy that need, and can make a profit from it is, by definition, marketing-oriented.

The purpose of this guide is to help Guild members become marketing-oriented, for these are the companies which grow and become successful.

▌SWOT Analysis

Every organisation has objectives, whether it is a large publicly quoted company anxious to increase its return on shareholders' funds, or a small local charity seeking to raise money for a new kidney dialysis machine. Their success or failure will depend upon their ability to define a cohesive strategy to achieve their objectives, and the implementation of that strategy.

In developing a corporate strategy, it makes sense to consider the Strengths and Weaknesses of the organisation and the Opportunities and Threats which confront it. This is often referred to as a SWOT analysis, an essential first step in the construction of any marketing plan.

Consider, for example, a jobbing builder with a small, highly skilled workforce of ageing professionals. He has no overdraft, limited cash resources, and a small borrowing facility at the bank. His SWOT analysis might begin as shown below.

Strengths
Skilled workers
Personal service
Competitive
Quick response
No overdraft

Weaknesses
Small company
Limited backup
Ageing workforce
Few repeat customers

Opportunities
Small jobs others refuse
Sub-contract work
Home improvements
Repairs and refurbishment

Threats
Small bank balance
Limited borrowing opportunities
Almost irreplaceable skills

From these few entries it is obvious that this builder should be seeking to satisfy a need for highly skilled work with regular staged payments, and that his pricing policy should allow for the fact that the 'product' he sells is in limited supply, and likely to become more so. In the longer term, if his business is to survive, he will have to find a way to replace the skills of his workers or consider a change in the direction of his business altogether.

Before going any further, why not draft out a SWOT analysis for your organisation? Do not spend a lot of time on it at this stage, but add to it as you continue to read this book, and as other ideas come to you. When you are satisfied that you have included as much as you can, discuss it with your accountant or other professional adviser. Tell him or her the story of you and your business and wait for a response, then redraft your SWOT analysis and consider the decisions that flow from it. This is a crucial first step in the preparation of any marketing plan.

The Marketing Environment

You should also be aware that outside the organisation there are many factors which can affect performance and profitability. These include:

- an increase or decrease in bank interest rates
- a change in the rate of VAT
- an amendment to the standard rate of Income Tax
- economic pressure on spending habits
- an international incident such as a war or revolution

More localised influences might be:

- a new competitor with a more competitive pricing structure
- a change in safety regulations or other standards
- changes in fashion and habit
- fluctuations in raw material supplies or prices
- new local authority costs or regulations

These, and many other factors outside the control of the business, take place within the marketing environment. It is imperative that every businessman is aware of them. The businessperson who does not keep up with trade and national press - even if only to skim through it - may well remain unaware of important news and information which could play a part in the successful implementation of his or her marketing plan.

The Marketing Audit

All businesses are aware of the financial audit: the historical assessment of a company's financial performance by a professionally qualified independent outsider. A marketing audit is somewhat different. It is a systematic internal appraisal and review of current marketing objectives and strategies, which highlights differences and variances from the marketing plan. Apart from enabling improvements to be made in the future, it helps to identify where there are differences between what people believe to be happening and what is actually happening.

The marketing audit makes it easier to carry out a performance review which will highlight where events were better or worse than expected. This will allow management to make changes to improve profitability before the current marketing plan has expired.

The marketing audit operates on two levels:

1 In the wider sense it looks at changes taking place outside the company, within the marketing environment, and considers their impact, for good or ill, on the performance of the business. For instance, what is the likely effect on the business if there has been a change in bank interest rates, and what changes will have to be made to the marketing plan?

2 Closer to home it concerns itself with matters within the business, such as specific performance levels, and compares them (possibly by ratios or indices) with the marketing plan, making recommendations for improved performance. This could be put into effect in any number of ways: increasing sales, improving the enquiry levels from current advertising, reducing the company's dependence on specific suppliers or customers, and many more.

Whether or not you have ever previously considered a marketing audit, it would be wise to make notes right now on your current marketing activity and performance, however limited they may be. Then, as you read through the following chapters you can consider some of the suggestions for improvement which may help you later in the preparation of your own comprehensive marketing plan.

▌ The Marketing-Oriented Company

Because marketing is concerned with providing the customer with what he wants, at a profit, it goes to the very heart of a company's operations. A marketing-oriented company is one which appreciates this fact and seeks to emphasise this concern for the customer in the products or services it offers at every level of activity.

This shows up in the way the business appears to its customers, from the way the telephone is answered, to writing a letter and presenting a quotation, to delivery of the goods on the promised date. Good impressions attract customers' attention. For example, a driver who delivers your products may believe that he works for your Transport Department. But if he is courteous and polite, anxious to make a good impression on the customers he meets, he is obviously aware of his marketing responsibilities and probably works for a marketing-oriented company.

Marketing cannot operate in a vacuum. The first people who need to understand this are those who work in the business; then come distributors and dealers. There is absolutely no point in telling customers how much you appreciate their business when your company does not brief staff on products, allows telephones to ring without being answered, fails to take messages and return calls, and dismisses customers' concerns as irrelevant.

▌Training

Training is part of the first line of marketing communications. Without it your personnel cannot help spread the message you are spending a lot of time and money creating. Any company intending to become marketing-oriented will recognise the importance of staff training at every level. The girl on the switchboard and the packer in the warehouse, as much as the salesman face-to-face with a customer, should be aware of the position they occupy in the marketing chain. They should all understand the importance of customer contact, from the first telephone enquiry to delivery of the products ordered; from taking down an order to handling a complaint. This will not happen through wishful thinking, nor even a management directive; it should be the end result of a planned, well-executed and ongoing training programme.

SUMMARY

▌ Marketing is the profitable satisfaction of a customer need.

▌ Marketing begins with an analysis of a company's:

Strengths and Weaknesses
Opportunities and Threats

in short, a SWOT analysis.

▌ The marketing environment exists outside the organisation.
What happens there can have an impact on sales and profits.

▌ A marketing audit assesses current marketing activity and considers
changes to improve future performance.

▌ A marketing audit looks at the wider marketing environment as
well as specific marketing performance inside the company.

▌ A marketing-oriented company places customer satisfaction at the
centre of its activities.

▌ All employees require training in order to appreciate the
importance of their position in the marketing chain.

2 What Planning Achieves

Business, like everything else in life, contains an element of risk. You can improve the odds of getting it right and slant them in your direction - but you cannot eliminate risk entirely.

Facts and information help you make decisions. With them, you can reduce risk and improve the probability of making the right decision. Preparation is vital, and anyone trying to promote a product or service should realise this. Actions taken in the planning stage should anticipate the need for investment and measure the likely return on that investment.

One of the most important investments this book should identify for you is the time and effort needed to prepare a proper marketing plan. Some will find this irksome, and an unnecessary expenditure of valuable resources which could be better employed in making a product or developing a service. Others will see it as simply another excuse for delaying getting on with the real work. They are both wrong.

Observe the construction of a tall building. The first and subsequent floors follow quite quickly when the foundations have been laid. But look at the work that precedes them: digging the foundations, getting them level, ensuring they are firm enough. The best plans are built on a solid base.

A plan is not a blueprint. It is a guide. It should keep you pointing the way you want to go, and inform you when you are going wrong so that corrective action can be taken. The planning process begins by looking at your business.

▌What Business Are You In?

Marketing experts will tell you that most of the large independent railway companies that dominated the business world at the turn of the century eventually died because they did not realise what business they were in. They thought they were in the railroad business when, in fact, they were in the transportation business. Had they realised this, they would not have remained within the narrow confines of their own industry but would have expanded into sea and air transportation - as Canadian Pacific did, for instance.

This is, of course, a great oversimplification, but there is an element of truth in it. A builder who builds individual extensions on domestic premises may believe he is in the building business, and may feel that his job is simply to follow instructions given by the homeowner. There is absolutely nothing wrong with this, but the same builder believing he is in the business of home improvement would keep himself informed of new products for the home and new ideas and new ways of improvement, which he could expect to find in the trade press. He could then improve his own business by offering advice and suggestions to a customer who would almost certainly be less well-informed in these matters than he is.

▌ Looking at Yourself

Self-criticism is not easy; too much of it can also be harmful and destructive. Constructive criticism is what we are looking for, and if we are prepared to look at what is wrong in what we do, let us do it in a way which will help us recognise our faults and find ways to correct them. We can start by looking at your business exactly as a new customer would find it.

The first contact a potential customer has with your business is probably through an advertisement, a leaflet or letter of introduction. What does he find? You may have kept the design of your advertisements and stationery for a number of years. Do they look old? Would they make a potential customer think that you are behind the times? Are they printed well? Is the Guild logo in the corner recognisable for what it is?

Assuming the customer writes in, how promptly is the letter answered? It may be a quick response when you are around, but what happens if you are sick or on holiday? It isn't difficult for someone to send a letter advising that the complaint/query/estimate request, or whatever, will be dealt with as soon as you return.

If the contact is made by telephone, how is it answered? Is it prompt? Is it polite? A pharmaceutical company in Berkshire was always so quick to answer the telephone that regular callers knew they had to be alert and ready with their requests. As a result, very little time was wasted and all calls went through quickly.

Looking at your business in this way can be a very constructive exercise. It should follow right through from submitting an estimate, meeting the customer and checking the quality of service or products provided to invoicing, payment and follow-up. You can even give yourself marks out of ten for each section and make

periodic reviews to see if your overall performance is improving or deteriorating.

▌ Looking at Your Competitors

It may help to see your business in a new light if you also look closely at your competitors. Perhaps it is possible to measure them on the same scale to see how they compare. This can be particularly helpful when considering adjustments to your prices. If others are providing a lesser quality service at higher prices whilst still obtaining sufficient work, perhaps you can safely increase your prices without the risk of losing too many of your existing customers. However, it is important that your judgements are as objective as possible and supported by independent third party observations where possible.

SUMMARY

■ In business you can never eliminate risk entirely although you can weigh the odds in your favour.

■ Facts and information increase the probability of making the right decision.

■ The best plans are those which have been well prepared and researched.

■ The business you are in may not be quite as narrow and confining as you first think.

■ It helps to look at your business through the eyes of your customers at all points where you interact.

■ It should be possible to measure your performance and make periodic checks for signs of improvement or otherwise.

■ Competitors' performances may also be evaluated on the same scale and compared directly with your own.

■ Judgements of competitors' performance should be supported by independent third party observation where possible.

3 Aspects of Marketing

Because we, as individuals, have different ways of expressing our need for the same or similar products, any manufacturer or distributor attempting to sell these products must necessarily find different ways of marketing to us. For example, a car dealer selling the same model car to me, as an individual, and you, as a car hire company, will stress different features and benefits to satisfy our needs. In addition, whereas his initial message could have been relayed to me through a newspaper or Sunday supplement, his point of contact with you is more likely to be a trade magazine or a personal call from a Sales Representative.

Before commencing any marketing programme, the medium and the message must be considered in the light of the potential customers we are hoping to reach.

▍Consumer Marketing

When marketing to the general public, we have a natural inclination to think of mass markets: avid followers of 'Coronation Street' or readers of the

Daily Mirror. This is not always so: a door-to-door salesman, a mail drop to a select group of householders, or even an advertisement in the local church magazine all come under the heading of consumer marketing.

The message used can be as varied as the potential size of the audience. A distributor of swimming pool supplies will concern himself only with those houses in a town likely to possess their own pool. His sales message can therefore be much more personal and direct than a 30-second soap powder commercial on TV.

Costs can vary greatly as well. A leaflet mailed to households will cost around £150 per thousand for postage alone, even after making allowance for the most generous discounts. A full-page advertisement which is likely to be seen by most of the *Daily Mail's* 1.8 million readers will cost just over £15 per thousand, but will still set you back £27,500 in total.

The decision on how to market your product or service to consumers will therefore depend on many factors, not the least of which is the nature of the product or service itself. Some products lend themselves more to mass marketing, others require a more personal approach. But most of all, the choice revolves around targeting and wastage. The size of the total audience is important but not overriding. Most important is the number of potential purchasers - those actually able and likely to buy. And this applies to the local church magazine as much as to the *Daily Mail*.

▌Industrial Marketing

Any businessman knows that he requires more information about the products he needs to run his business than those he buys for domestic use only. It could be, for example, that he ends up choosing the same calculator for home and office use. But whereas with the former his requirements are simple addition and subtraction, he would not have bought the calculator for office use if it did not have the statistical functions he requires. That is why industrial marketing is, generally speaking, more technical than consumer marketing.

The industrial customer is different, too. He is more likely to be objective and dispassionate in his purchasing decisions. This means that he is more likely to be swayed by facts rather than emotion, and to consider long-term cost considerations over short-term satisfaction.

Frequently these facts are best presented by personal sales representation. The role of the sales representative can be extremely important when selling to industrial customers. Personal selling is a two-way form of communication which allows the potential purchaser to ask difficult or technical questions before making a decision. However, personal selling is very expensive, and that is why the quality of representation is so important for companies marketing to industrial customers.

▌Retail Marketing

A retailer is a middleman. His position in the marketing chain is usually between the wholesaler and the consumer, and sometimes between the manufacturer and the consumer. In either case he receives a sales message from the wholesaler or manufacturer which, hopefully, he will then relay to the consumer. Because of the number of products the retailer has to sell, this is not always possible. It is therefore crucial that anyone wishing to sell his products through the retail trade should give as much assistance as possible to the retailer himself.

This help can be given in a number of different ways. Rather than expecting the retailer to 'push' your products to his customers, you can 'pull' your products through his shop by creating a demand. This demand can be the result of consumer advertising, extra discounts which allow the retailer to reduce prices without sacrificing margin, or point-of-sale material which encourages the consumer to ask for your products off the shelf.

Advertising to the retailer is almost always through trade magazines.

▌ Export Marketing

Domestic marketing campaigns are rarely exportable without substantial changes. Tastes, attitudes and social customs associated with culture, tradition or religious practices can change dramatically at national boundaries. That is why considerable thought and preparation are required before attempting to market products and services to another country.

The history of marketing is full of horrendous mistakes made by companies who thought they could sell their products overseas without local knowledge and professional advice. No language is literally translatable into another without humorous or tragic consequences; religious symbols mean different things to different people, and even colours which have happy associations in one culture can mean completely the reverse in another.

Apart from cultural taboos, there are many legal restrictions and trade and tariff barriers erected by governments. It therefore makes sense to consult experts who know and understand these problems.

▌A Rose by Another Name?

Last year an English company was planning a mailing to a large number of homes in Finland. Unfortunately, in translating the text the Finnish letter 'Ø', with a slash, became the English letter 'O', without one, changing the meaning of one word quite dramatically. Instead of being offered the holiday home of a lifetime, Finnish consumers found that they were being given the opportunity to purchase a very private part of the body.

The error was widely broadcast in the Finnish media, but the advertiser had the last laugh. A follow-up mailing, boldly stating 'As featured on TV' more than doubled the anticipated response.

SUMMARY

▌ Different marketing techniques are required for selling the same products to industrial and consumer markets.

▌ Consumer marketing is not necessarily the same thing as mass marketing.

▌ When considering marketing costs, think of the number of potential purchasers rather than the total audience in any particular advertising medium.

▌ Industrial customers usually require more technical information than most consumers.

▌ The role of the sales representative is particularly important in industrial marketing.

▌ To get the best from retailers, assistance should be provided when attempting to sell your products through retail outlets.

▌ There are many potential pitfalls to be avoided when marketing products overseas.

▌ Tastes, attitudes and social customs, legal restrictions and trade and tariff barriers must all be considered when marketing in other countries.

4 The Market

A sales manager of a large garment manufacturing company used to have a big sign behind his desk which was immediately visible to all visitors. It read, 'Nothing Happens Until Somebody Sells Something.' In a sense, he was quite right, for although all business activity starts with an idea, nothing really happens until that idea is sold to someone. It is that someone, rather than the activity, which concerns us here. What we are looking for is a market receptive to our ideas.

▌Identifying a Need

There is an old marketing adage that says: 'When a man buys a drill, he does not want a drill - he wants a hole.' This is another way of saying that everybody who needs a hole is in the market for a drill. Or, to put it yet another way, the market for a drill is the people who need a hole.

Psychologists tell us that there is a whole hierarchy of needs which begins with the basic needs for food and shelter and progresses through a series of stages to videos and compact disc players - what we know as luxury goods.

The same thing applies to business needs. Many large and well-known companies started out as a one-man-business in an old workshop or garage. At that time the need for a typewriter did not seem paramount. Today, it is quite possible that these same companies supply personal computers to most of their office staff (and even laptop computers to their salesforce) because they are essential for performing duties properly.

Needs are not the same thing as demand, although one may follow the other. In the 1950s and 1960s it was the need for warm homes, rather than warm rooms heated by individual fires, which created the demand for central heating. Plumbers and small builders who were quick to recognise this and organise themselves accordingly reaped the greatest rewards.

Identifying a Market

A market is a group of customers with a single, identifiable need. Some of these could be heavy or regular users of your products; others will be light or infrequent purchasers.
Recognising the difference can be important for your marketing efforts.

It is frequently claimed (and supported by research) that 80% of the purchases of any particular product come from just 20% of the customers. Those marketing to consumers often concentrate their efforts on heavy purchasers. It is generally believed that it is easier to sell something to those who are already committed users of the product.

Direct mail advertisers know that the greatest response can be expected from those who have purchased by mail order in the past. That is why most companies go to great lengths to build up a database of customers who may be contacted when special promotions and incentives are offered.

It is worth mentioning at this point that there can be more than a pedantic difference between a customer and a consumer. A customer may well be making a purchase on behalf of another. Examples include the industrial buyer purchasing materials to manufacture products sold to consumers, retailers buying products for resale to consumers, and even the housewife purchasing groceries for her family. In each case it is the customer's perception of the consumer's needs which most influences the buying decision.

Segmenting a Market

Markets can be segmented in a number of different ways. Consider a brewer introducing a new beer on the market. Before the launch he could look at the total beer market in a number of different ways. He might distinguish those who buy a particular brand because they like the taste, those who are mostly concerned with quenching their thirst, and those who consider the alcohol content - whether high or low - most important.

After looking at the different market segments, their growth or decline over recent years and the strength of the competition in each, he would be in a better position to make a reasonable assessment of the profitability of each segment and then make a decision on the advertising and promotional bias for the introduction of his new product.

A cabinetmaker supplying fitted furniture units to individual households might discover, purely by chance, an unexpectedly high demand for his skills at the top end of the market, in the higher income bracket. Because of this he might concentrate a direct mail campaign to the most exclusive homes in his area.

Markets can be segmented in a number of different ways. The important thing to note is that the criteria for segmentation must be relevant to the buying decision. There is little point in identifying potential left-handed customers (assuming this were possible) if left-handedness made no difference whatsoever to the decision whether or not to buy.

In addition, the segment chosen must be of sufficient size to warrant attention and should not be too difficult to contact with your promotion, nor too difficult to supply with your products.

The benefits of segmentation can be quite considerable - they usually reduce competition, create closer identity with customers and increase the opportunities to improve profits.

▌Segmentation in Practice

A member of the Guild of Master Craftsmen wrote in, requesting help in writing a direct mail letter. His business was in welding, but he had discovered a special demand which he could satisfy: constructing boarding kennels for animals. His kennels were secure, light and airy, guaranteed to return a happy pet to a satisfied owner. Animal boarding kennels represented a market segment which he could identify and target. We supplied a letter aimed at this new market.

Another member of the Guild, a small plumber, also wanted help with a direct mail letter. The market segment he had identified consisted of near-neighbours who had small jobs which would not be of interest to larger competitors. He knew where these potential customers lived. The letter we supplied told them of his interest in the work.

SUMMARY

■ Customer needs are not the same as demand, although one may follow the other.

■ 80% of the purchases of any particular product come from 20% of the customers.

■ It is usually easier to sell to committed users of a product.

■ Customers make purchases on behalf of consumers in anticipation of their perceived needs.

■ Markets can be segmented in a number of different ways.

■ The criteria for segmentation must be relevant to the buying decision.

■ The benefits of segmentation can be considerable.

5 The Product

Without a product or service to sell, you would not have a business. The whole purpose of business is to make and sell products, at a profit. When talking of products, we do not mean simply their physical characteristics - their nuts and bolts - we mean the total package inherent in every product, including its price, availability, reputation etc.

It is not enough to think of one aspect of a product in isolation. Price is important, but if everyone bought on price alone there would be no place for the Rolls-Royce, Harrods, or even Marks & Spencer.

Every product is more than the sum of its physical parts. As soon as a brand name is stamped upon it, it changes - some customers will think for the better, others the reverse. Time after time, blind tests - where the consumer is unaware of the brand of product he or she is assessing - display different results to open tests with the same products, branded. The added ingredient is the brand image, whether it be good, bad or indifferent.

▌What We Are Selling

Sales managers are frequently heard encouraging their salesmen to 'sell the sizzle and not the steak'. This is good marketing advice. If we stop to consider our marketing definition, we have to think of our products satisfying a customer need. This means that we have to think of the needs of our customers and the way our products satisfy these needs.

Consider, for a moment, a husband and wife deciding whether, or from whom, they should buy a new fitted kitchen. They will first ask themselves if they really need one. The wife might say yes, wondering how she has managed with her old, out-of-date kitchen for so long. The husband might ask if a new kitchen should take priority over a new garage. Having made the decision that it does, they will probably then ask themselves how much they can afford to spend and what new appliances they can include for the money - possibly a microwave, which they have never had before, but have heard one of their neighbours praise so highly. They will consider the timescale - could the new kitchen be installed before Christmas? They will think of the disruption and mess - does the supplier have skilled workers who will clean up afterwards? All these questions and answers form part of the continuing process we call consumer buyer behaviour.

Who, then, is likely to obtain the order from our fictitious (but nevertheless typical) couple? Presumably all the companies they contact are able to supply fitted kitchens. But only one will best meet their requirements for a kitchen which is within their budget, fitted with the appliances they require (probably allowing a special discount on the microwave they have set their hearts on), with generous repayment terms, installed before Christmas by skilled, efficient, neat and tidy craftsmen.

▌Enhancing the Product

In the previous section, we outlined a number of ways of segmenting a market and the opportunities available to those who successfully do so. One way to segment a market is to enhance your product, or add value to it - in other words, make it different from the competition.

A product can be enhanced by adding extra features, new improved ingredients, better quality materials and so on. It can be improved by the efficiency of your switchboard, the help and advice given by your salesmen, the accuracy of your estimates etc. Value is added when you offer concessionary repayment terms, provide discounted bonus 'gifts' or offer faster settlement terms.

The point is not that *all* of these features should be offered to prospective customers or that some of them should not be standard in every package you offer. The main thing to remember is that, whatever products or services you sell, they are not bought or sold in isolation. They are part of a package of benefits. And the more these benefits correspond with the needs of your customers, the more successful you will be in selling them.

▌Changing the Product

There comes a time in the life of most products when they go into decline. Marketing handbooks talk of 'Product Lifecycles' which begin with the introduction to the market and progress through growth, maturity, saturation and decline. Some lifecycles last longer than others. The petrol-driven motor car has been with us for quite a long time and is, today, an integral part of our lives. But if we try to project our imaginations forward a hundred years, could we honestly expect it to remain so? It is more than likely that it will have been replaced by a completely new mode of transportation powered by a different source of energy.

The same thing applies to services. Mens' hairdressers as we know them have been around for many years and, on the premise that men will continue to have their hair cut regularly, are likely to do so far into the future. Yet there was a time during the 1960s and 1970s when mens' hairdressers looked particularly vulnerable to a long-haired fashion that forced many of them out

of business. And who is to say what will happen to fashion in the future?

Every business has to adapt to new and changing times in order to survive. The really successful businesses, however, seize the opportunities change brings. When the sales of automatic washing machines began to take off, an entrepreneurial plumber would have grasped the opportunity to advise all households in his area of the excellent service he could provide in plumbing them in. An especially entrepreneurial plumber might also have approached the management of shops selling white goods, offering his services to customers purchasing automatic washing machines. How much easier it would be for the retail salesman if he could sell the product with the added benefit of a reputable and reliable plumber, willing and able to plumb in the new machine for a fixed and agreed price.

Changing a product or service in response to customer needs is *essential* for any business which wants to grow and prosper.

SUMMARY

■ A product is much more than the sum of its physical parts.

■ Every product or service is a package of benefits which includes its price, availability, reputation etc.

■ The product is more successful the closer its benefits correspond to the needs of consumers.

■ Product enhancement is a means of segmenting a market.

■ A product can be enhanced in many different ways and its perceived value increased.

■ For every product there is a lifecycle.

■ Products are introduced to the market and progress through periods of growth, maturity, saturation and decline.

■ Businesses must adapt their products to meet the demands of changing times in order to survive.

■ Successful businesses seize the opportunities change offers.

6 The Right Price

In your opinion, what is the right price for a pint of bitter? Or, if you prefer, what is the right price for a half-pound bar of milk chocolate? As far as the customer is concerned, the answers vary, not only from individual to individual but for the same individual at different times. Wouldn't we all be prepared to pay more for a chocolate bar when hungry, and more for a pint of bitter on a long, hot summer's day?

For the supplier, similar arguments apply. Most manufacturers would be ready to charge less for their products when stocks are high and demand low, and to charge more when stocks are low and demand high.

In truth, there is no such thing as a single, all-embracing 'right price' for any product, except what one supplier and one customer agree is right at one moment in time.

▌Profit Margins

Every business has its own way of identifying a profit margin.
In the pricing examples which follow, a number of methods of arriving at a price are given, and these are intended to ensure that there is a profit margin when the work is completed.
Whichever way you define margin, there has to be one. Without margin there is no profit, and without profit there could soon be no business.

When talking of profit margin, one of three things is usually meant:

1 Gross Margin - the selling price less all direct production costs.
2 Net Margin - gross margin less all overheads.
3 Net Profit - net margin less all finance costs.

Marginal Cost and Added Value

There is another aspect of margin which is of major importance - that of marginal cost or the cost of making one more. In very depressed trading conditions some companies will sell at, or slightly above, marginal cost in order just to pay wages and keep machines ticking over. In the very short term this can make sense, provided

- it is a one-off and does not set a pattern or annoy other customers
- it is presented as price less volume/loyalty/introductory discount
- it has no hidden costs such as special credit terms

The concept of marginal costing (as distinct from marginal pricing) can be useful in the longer term when related to added value. The level of pricing above marginal cost shows the added value or contribution to overheads made by the 'surplus' in the selling price. Properly monitored and controlled, it clearly illustrates the true effect of pricing decisions and the rate of overhead recovery in what may be a very competitive marketplace.

It is, of course, essential that gross margins, marginal costs and breakeven sales levels are known, and that these are monitored continuously, analysed and verified each month.

Cost-Plus

When fixing a price for a product or service, many suppliers apply some variation of cost-plus. They determine their costs as best they can, and then add on a percentage mark-up. It is a fairly simple formula to apply and, for an experienced businessman who keeps a close watch on material prices and can make a fairly accurate prediction of wage variations during the length of the contract, it can form the basis of 'off-the-cuff' estimates. But is it good enough? Are prices determined simply by costs and a 'satisfactory' profit level?

Pricing Objectives

Every company should have corporate objectives of one kind or another. These could be strictly financial (return on capital etc.), numerical (volume of sales) or size relative to competitors (market share). Pricing objectives should be related to these overall corporate objectives - there is no point in adopting a cost-plus pricing policy, which totally ignores the prices charged by competitors, when the corporate objective is to realise or maintain a certain percentage market share.

▌Pricing Too Low

It is very easy to price low in order to obtain work. Some companies do this deliberately, particularly in difficult times, offering to undercut any other prices received. This can work, provided you are sure that your fixed costs are covered by the volume received and not the volume anticipated.

If you are able to manufacture 1,000 units a week and spread your overheads over this quantity, it will not help at all if you are only able to obtain orders for 800. Similarly, if you set an hourly rate spreading your overheads over 40 productive hours a week when you can only find work for 35 hours, you could soon be in serious trouble.

There are, of course, many good reasons for pricing low. It could be that you are trying to penetrate a new market where your reputation is unknown, and you may well need to offer a price incentive to succeed. Possibly you wish to offer a special promotional price to get a sluggish market sector moving again. Whatever the reason, you might be more successful if your prices do not fluctuate but you offer special concessionary discounts for volume, prompt payment, or even, perhaps, for the time of year the order is placed: a seasonal discount.

▌Pricing Too High

Every economist will tell you that there is a direct relationship between demand and price. He calls it a demand curve. In theory the higher the price, the lower the demand, and vice versa. It does not always work but has a certain logic which most of us can understand. It also follows that higher prices do not necessarily maximise profits: if a 10% reduction in

▌Difficult Pricing Decisions

An antique restorer, considering joining the Guild of Master Craftsmen, wrote in requesting help and advice about obtaining the right price for his craft. He felt that he was subject to intolerable pressures from his customers to keep his prices down whilst all around him he could see other prices increase. He was advised to make a special note on estimates and invoices of the amount of labour involved in his work and the hourly rate charged. This compared favourably with charges made by other less-skilled trades. He was given examples of other companies and businesses who have prospered despite charging above the expected market rate. More than anything else, though, it was suggested that he should not feel defensive about his pricing structure, as buyers who genuinely look for quality in the products they buy have a very different conception of the right price than the average 'bargain hunter'.

price produces a 50% increase in demand, profits will probably increase. Again, it all comes down to objectives. If you do not want your business to grow any larger, you may not wish to increase the demand for your products. But if you are not selling enough, either your sales message is wrong, it is not reaching the right people, or your prices are too high.

▌Pricing for Value

Whatever pricing decision is made, no one can afford to ignore the association in our minds between price and value. Although we all hope to find bargains when we shop, it is generally true that we believe high prices mean quality and very low prices mean junk. If prices are set too high or too low, this can affect customers' perceptions of the position of the product in the marketplace, and this can be more important for the future of a business than winning or losing a particular order.

SUMMARY

■ The right price is the one both buyer and seller agree upon.

■ Pricing at marginal cost during depressed trading conditions may make sense in the very short term.

■ With cost-plus pricing it is essential to ensure that demand is sufficient to cover fixed and variable costs.

■ Pricing objectives should be strictly related to overall company objectives.

■ Discounts can be offered for volume, prompt payment or off-season placement of order.

■ Discounts may convince a customer that a better bargain is being offered.

■ High prices do not necessarily mean that profits are maximised.

■ There is a definite correlation between price and value for most customers.

■ Pricing too high or too low can adversely affect product positioning in the market place.

7 Selling The Product

For those who have never been involved in personal selling, this can appear a daunting prospect. But selling is not always as difficult as we expect it to be. In real life most of us are selling ourselves all the time, without even realising it. And despite popular belief, the fast-talking, wisecracking extrovert does not always make the best salesman. More often the soft-spoken, sincere individual, selling a product or service which he genuinely believes will benefit his customer, is far more effective.

The secret of successful selling is knowing the product. Product knowledge brings confidence, and a confident salesman will soon enjoy the trust of his customers and, no matter what is being sold, the sale is effectively made only when the customer begins to trust the salesman.

Most professional salesmen will tell you that they are not selling at all. They are helping the customer to buy. They present the advantages and disadvantages of their products in specific situations, and demonstrate to their customer how these products will satisfy his needs. The accent is upon helpfulness rather than persuasion. The old-fashioned salesman with the slap on the back and the funny story is being replaced by the committed professional with a genuine desire to help his customer.

▌Personal Selling

But why bother with salesmen at all, you might ask? If my work is good enough, satisfied customers will become my salesforce; new customers will come to me automatically. There is some truth in this. Although it is doubtful that the world will beat a pathway to your door if you build a better mousetrap, there is no doubt that, for example, a small workshop of specialist craftsmen could prosper without any sales people at all. More likely, though, in situations like this, the principals are salesmen without even realising it. They are handling objections, answering queries, closing the sale and following up after the work is completed - everything a good salesman would do as a matter of course.

The First Impression

But where does the sale begin? It begins immediately contact is made with the prospect. It could be a personal introduction, a letter, a telephone call, or a direct approach in a customer's home or office. No matter where it is, or what the circumstance, the impression made at that first contact will dictate the course of the sale. And that first impression will last for a long, long time.

If a salesman tries to ingratiate himself with his prospect by relating personal or business information obtained from other customers, the prospect will expect the salesman to be equally free with his confidential information. If the contact is by letter and the letterheading is untidy or otherwise poorly presented, this is the image the prospect will have of the salesman and the company he represents.

It may all sound like basic commonsense - and it is! Yet how often is a salesmen heard criticising the work of a competitor to a prospect, even when he knows that the prospect has previously bought from that same competitor. The salesman probably does not stop to think what he is saying. If he did, he would realise that he is, in effect, calling his prospect a fool for buying from the wrong supplier. If there is an art in salesmanship, it consists of the salesman always putting himself in the position of his customer.

Sales Methodology

Sales manuals will tell you that there are four basic steps in the selling process; often referred to as AIDA. The first is attracting the Attention of the sales prospect, the second is obtaining his Interest in what you have to sell, the third is arousing a Desire in your prospect in what you have to sell, and the fourth is stimulating Action, or closing the sale. However, like all simplified procedures, this in no way covers all the activities of a fully-trained professional salesman.

Whilst it is true that a good salesman instinctively responds to the needs of his customers, if he is truly competent he will ensure that he approaches his work following a number of basic steps. These include:

1 Searching out and finding new sales prospects.
2 Adapting his sales message to the needs of a particular customer.
3 Helping the customer make the right choice - that is, helping him to buy.
4 Giving the prospect good advice.
5 Answering specific questions and overcoming objections.
6 Reassuring the customer with doubts about a particular point.
7 Demonstrating the benefits of his product.
8 Helping uncertain customers make up their minds.
9 Asking for the order - that is, closing the sale.
10 Making the customer aware of complementary products which could increase the value of the sale.
11 Finding out if the customer is in the market for other products in the range.
12 Following up after the sale to ensure that the customer is satisfied.

▍Closing the Sale

The most difficult part of any sales presentation for the inexperienced salesperson is closing the sale. That is why salesmen are frequently and rightly criticised for talking too much. They do not know how to end the presentation so they go on and on and on, almost trying to tire the customer into submission. You will probably have experienced this yourself at one time or another.

There is only one way of closing a sales presentation, and that is to ask for the order. There are a number of ways of doing this. The direct approach is a straightforward question: 'Are you ready to place your order now?' Another is to assume that you have the order and simply pass the order form and a pen to the customer, asking for his signature. More subtle approaches include offering your customer two or three alternatives and asking which one he would prefer or, if your product comes in different sizes and colours, asking if the red one is preferred or if the one litre size is most suitable.

The Hidden Objection

No salesman is successful every time. For some customers it really is the wrong product, the wrong time or the wrong price, but many sales are lost because the salesman never gets to hear the hidden objection.

During any sales presentation the prospect is certain to offer objections. In most cases he will be looking for reassurance. If he claims that he is worried that you may not be able to deliver on time, he may simply be looking for some guarantee from you that your delivery promises will be kept. But if he has heard from a disgruntled customer that your quality is suspect, he may hold back from telling you. And if it worries him enough, he will offer some other reason for his unwillingness to place an order: 'The price is too high' or 'I can't afford it at the moment' are two of the favourites. The awful truth is that if you knew of the hidden objection you could probably answer it.

So, how do you go about finding the hidden objection your prospect seems so concerned to keep to himself? One of the world's most successful salesman, Frank Bettger, came up with the answer. His tried and tested procedure involved saying: 'But in addition to that, is there some other reason why you do not want to place an order.' In his experience, this simple sentence drew out the hidden objection time and time again. And once you have learned what it is, you are then in a position to answer it - before, hopefully, going on to close the sale.

Ongoing Relationships

It has been said that the difference between the salesman and the confidence trickster is that the salesman is welcomed back. And, as many good salesmen will tell you, they frequently become friends with their customers. It is all part of building an ongoing relationship.

The amount of contact any salesman has with his customers will vary with the nature of the business. A print salesman is likely to make more calls on any one customer than a life assurance salesman. But the latter should always maintain some contact, even if it consists of a Christmas card and the occasional telephone call. You never know when new business may be around the corner or a recommendation is there simply for the asking.

▌Sales Opportunities

In every business it is almost always true that the greatest source of new business comes from existing customers. Satisfied customers return time and time again. In addition, they frequently recommend good suppliers to friends and acquaintances. That is why good salesmen will always ask satisfied customers if they know of anyone else who might benefit from their products or services. Introductions are far, far more effective than cold calls.

SUMMARY

■ Fast-talking, wisecracking extroverts do not always make the best salesmen.

■ The sale is made only when the customer begins to trust the salesman.

■ A soft-spoken, sincere salesman, selling a product he believes in, achieves the best results.

■ Knowing the product is the secret of successful selling.

■ Good salesmen actually help their customers to buy.

■ A successful sales presentation consists of attracting attention, obtaining interest, arousing desire and stimulating action to close the sale.

■ Knowing how and when to close the sale is extremely important.

■ If your prospect will not buy, look for the hidden objection.

■ Generally speaking, the greatest source of new business comes from existing customers.

■ Recommendations from satisfied customers are the best sales prospects.

8 Choosing The Right Channel

Marketing is more than simply developing, pricing and promoting a product. In order to achieve optimum sales, that product must be made available in the right place at the right time. Selecting the channels through which to sell and distribute products is a marketing responsibility.

It may seem at first that distribution channels are fairly static. It is only when we stop to consider the changes in retailing over the last few years and the changes that have taken place in distribution that we can begin to understand the dynamics of channel management and the new demands made on marketing managers. Just one example: who would have thought ten years ago that petrol stations would today be selling sandwiches, confectionery, music cassettes and discs, magazines and daily newspapers, flowers, watering cans, and even Christmas trees - to name just a few of the many items they now sell in addition to petrol and oil?

Manufacturers, importers and agents must be constantly alert to the changes taking place in distribution and the opportunities and threats they represent to existing successful companies.

▌Distribution Levels

When deciding to place a product in a particular market, the distribution coverage is a prime consideration. Many companies, especially when launching a new product, will look for intensive distribution, where anyone prepared to handle the product is allowed to do so. Others look to selective distribution, where only those outlets likely to do a good job for the product are given the necessary approval. Depending upon the product, some others will look for exclusive distribution where just one middleman is given exclusive rights to sell the product in a certain area. (These areas sometimes can be whole countries or even continents.)

When discussing distribution, the manufacturer will want to know the quality of the distributor's reputation and representation: how well can the distributor push the product through the channel? The distributor, on the other hand, will want to know the manufacturer's plans for advertising and promotion: how much assistance can the distributor expect to pull the product through the channel?

Amongst distributors there are specialists and, if your product is interesting to them, they will take it on and promote it. When entering a distribution agreement make sure that if the distributor wants exclusivity, he has to make commitments to move agreed volumes within agreed timescales and accept that his failure to do so will cost him his exclusivity.

A special point to note about such a relationship is that you should always communicate in writing all matters relating to the agreement. If there is a breach of the agreement, do something about it rather than just hoping that it will resolve itself. If you do not act, you may be setting an alternative deal by default. You can always write expressing the view that, whilst you recognise the shortfall or whatever, and you are prepared to tolerate it in this instance, this in no way changes the contractual terms of your agreement.

Channel management is a fast-changing business area in which manufacturers, importers and agents must be constantly alert to the changes taking place and the opportunities and threats they represent to many existing successful companies.

Transportation

Not so many years ago, the majority of goods in this country were distributed largely by rail. This has now changed so that road transportation is favoured, and today it is possible to obtain from several specialist carriers bulk rates for daily collection and a variety of delivery options to anywhere in mainland UK. These can be surprisingly low, and the firms offer a professional door-to-door service much preferred by customers.

In the future it is quite possible that environmental pressures, parking restrictions in inner cities and other considerations will bring further changes for manufacturers and wholesalers distributing products to retailers in High Street locations.

Retail Outlets

Nowhere have changes in shopping habits been more evident than in the traditional High Street. Many well-known names have disappeared in the last few years as new, fast-moving competitors have taken their business.

Some of these competitors have taken customers to new locations; out-of-town shopping centres, DIY superstores, hypermarkets and the rest. Department stores as we once knew them have almost disappeared, and those that survive have largely become stores-within-stores as smaller retail companies have taken over much of their floor space. The implications for those selling their products through these outlets can be very serious.

In the 1960s, a manufacturer of blue jeans gave the same discount to all his retail customers, no matter what level of purchases were made. His products were in demand, and because of his pricing policy he retained the loyalty of his many small rural customers, who were thus able to compete on price with the larger city stores. But as blue jeans became more popular and competitors offering volume discounts came on the market, his sales suffered, as the smaller rural customers were in low growth or declining population areas. The larger city stores were expanding fast. Within ten years the manufacturer had disappeared, taken over by one of his competitors. It was not his pricing policy itself that cost him his business, it was failing to understand the importance and relevance of channel management.

▌Direct-To-User

Although larger catalogue companies have tended to lose market share in recent years, smaller specialist catalogues have multiplied. Shops that offer goods from catalogues have appeared in the High Street, offering brand-named goods at discounted prices.

Telephone selling is on the increase, as is direct response from television advertising. Other methods of selling directly to the end user include direct mail, magazine and newspaper coupons, house parties, vending machines and exhibitions, to name just a few. All these affect the way goods are sold and distributed. No doubt others will appear in the future, offering new sales opportunities to those marketing managers with the vision and imagination to explore new and different methods of channelling their products to the consumer.

One of these will almost certainly be database marketing, where companies who at one time thought they were just selling goods to customers are now aware that they provide a service to named individuals. Thanks to the computer, it is now possible for these companies to contact their customers with special offers and promotions as often as they wish. Products which they once sold over the counter may now be distributed by mail or even delivered directly from the manufacturer, agent or importer.

SUMMARY

■ Products must be made available in the right place at the right time.

■ Marketing-oriented companies are constantly alert to the opportunities and threats offered by changes in distribution.

■ Distribution coverage for any product may be intensive, selective or exclusive.

■ Many traditional High Street shoppers now buy in quantity from out-of-town locations.

■ Department stores are becoming more stores-within-stores.

■ Telephone selling, television direct response and other new direct-to-user sales methods are bringing changes in distribution.

■ Database marketing will almost certainly create further changes in channel management.

9 Advertising

Advertising alone rarely sells products (although exceptions to this are direct response advertising and point-of-sale). It is part of the marketing mix and supports or supplements other marketing activities.

Advertising creates awareness. Two simple examples are products that move faster off the shelves if the brand name is recognised, and salesmen who find it easier to obtain sales from customers already aware of their company and the products they sell.

Information is conveyed through advertising. Price changes, product improvements and new distribution outlets can be relayed to customers through advertising. In fact, public announcements, financial and tender advertisements have no other objective than to pass on information.

Attitudes can be changed through advertising. Deeply entrenched attitudes are, of course, very difficult to change, but a sustained advertising programme, sometimes supported by endorsements from trustworthy public figures, can create fresh attitudes and help persuade customers that previous conceptions of a particular product were incorrect.

Advertisements also act as reminders to regular customers. With other advertising constantly vying for their attention, it is important that reminders are provided, even for products used regularly.

∎ The Beginning

Like most things in business, advertising achieves the best results when working to clearly defined, achievable objectives. The 'achievable' part is very important. A Rolls-Royce dealer might hope to sell ten of his cars through a single classified advertisement in the *Wellington Weekly Advertiser*, but it is extremely unlikely. The media selected, the size of the advertisement and the frequency of insertion must all be considered when setting the objectives for any advertising campaign.

▌ The Media

Opportunities for advertising are almost limitless. Wherever and whenever an audience can be assembled, someone will be prepared to advertise to it. Whether it is a crowd at a football match, readers of a particular publication or viewers of a certain television programme, they are all potential customers for some product or service. Advertising media fall into five broad categories:

1 Broadcast

Until fairly recently, the opportunities for advertising on radio and television were quite restricted. With the advent of satellite television and the introduction of a whole range of new specialist radio stations all around the country, this has now changed. Radio and television advertising is now an important and integral part of many advertising budgets of companies who would once have considered them too expensive.

2 Printed Publications

New magazines have been published with increasing frequency over recent years, so much so that most advertisers have to be very selective to ensure that the right publications are selected for promoting their products. The choice is very wide: there are national and regional, daily and weekly, free and paid for newspapers to consider, just for a start. Magazines are directed to the trade or the consumer and may be sold by subscription or on the newsstands or be distributed free of charge to selected readers. Then there are catalogues, directories, reference books, programmes and circulars.

3 Posters

Poster advertising is more than large 24-sheet posters on hoardings. There are cards for display in bus and train carriages - even inside taxicabs. There are exterior bus and taxi advertisements and posters for railway and underground stations. In this category we might also include outdoor signs of all kinds - painted, printed and illuminated. However, the

CREATORS OF FINE CUTLERY
◇ HALLMARKED SILVER ◇ SILVER PLATED ◇ STAINLESS STEEL ◇

THE
MARKS & SPENCER
1990
BETTER MADE IN BRITAIN
AWARD

United Cutlers of Sheffield

IN...

NUMBER OF PATTERN
SEE BACK PAGE.

RANGE AND QUALITY

Average pla...
Compatib...
Guarante...

MAIN TABLEWARE I...

Table Fork*	
Dessert Fork*	
Table Knife*	
Dessert Knife*	
Dessert Spoon*	
Soup Spoon*	
Tea Spoon*	
Serving Spoon	
Coffee Spoon	
Fish Fork	
Fish Knife	

SETS All sets can be m...

7 piece place set (items marked *)		521.00	800.00	52...
44 piece set (6 × 7 piece place sets and 2 serving spoons)		714.00	800.00	762.00	3,500.00
60 piece set (8 × 7 piece place sets and 4 serving spoons)		1,042.00	1,168.00		
88 piece set (12 × 7 piece place sets and 4 serving spoons)				

† Variations may occur due to silver finishing. Table & dessert knives have stainless steel blades.

CABINETS (Please specify finish when ordering)

MODEL	DIMENSIONS - CM	CAPACITY	PRICE
ST. ANN 86	26 × 31 × 13	**Up to 86 pieces:-** 8 × 7 piece sets, 8 prs fish eaters, 8 coffee spoons, 6 serving spoons.	£65
ST. ANN 126	45 × 30 × 11.5	**Up to 126 pieces:-** 12 × 7 piece sets, 12 prs fish eaters, 12 coffee spoons, 6 serving spoons.	£85
ST. ANN 195	45 × 50 × 17	**Up to 195 pieces:-** 12 × 7 piece sets, 12 prs fish eaters, 12 coffee spoons, 6 serving spoons, 3 piece carvers, 11 spare racks for another 66 pieces.	£130

... STERLING

...e are delighted to
...d sterling silver,
...cutlery rolls too.
...cutlery from £60
...member, THE
...ring July and

...say 'Up to'
...o ensure you

...ement your

...You will
...f. If you have time,
appear in the enclosed Price

...order form, remembering
...to complete both sides of
... — no postage stamp is
...t AUGUST – be sure

...for up to a lifetime of
...portant assurances of
...re dealing directly
...ery makers. Our

CABINETS

Our hand crafted cabinets are beautifully made and represent excellent value for money. They are available in 3 sizes (see table) and in 3 finishes – MAHOGANY, DARK OAK and NATURAL OAK. Please denote the size and finish you require on your order.

Conscious of our environmental responsibilities, we insist upon our timber supplies being drawn only from countries and companies which have good re-forestation policies.

David Collins
Chief Executive

...charge card holders may telephone their orders during
...business hours, or fax them to us at any time. But be quick –
don't miss the 31st August deadline.

P.P.S. Please do not hesitate to contact us if you have a query or require
any assistance whatsoever. We are here to help you.

biggest growth in this area has been the use of posters at televised sports events - there are specialist brokers whose expertise is knowing just where the camera points most often. There are even rotating poster displays so that three advertisers can share a spot at the side of the pitch.

4 Novelty

The catch-all category of novelty advertising includes pencils, T-shirts, balloons, calendars, coasters and many others too varied to be listed separately.

5 Sponsorship

It is difficult to think of many sports today without their direct sponsorship: soccer, tennis, cricket, golf, motor racing and many others rely heavily on the income received from sponsors anxious to have their name seen by spectators, or viewers at home watching the event on television. Some sporting events' organisers also obtain considerable extra revenue from hospitality facilities provided, and even school sporting events can benefit from local sponsorship.

▌The Message

Having chosen the medium to carry the advertisement, is there any best way for the advertiser to present his message? In a way, the answer is no, but in another way, the answer is yes. There are certain rules to be followed when planning the creative side of an advertisement, but if there was one definitive way that always worked, everyone would do it. Many very sophisticated companies spend tens of thousands of pounds every year on advertisements that do not work. They do not do it deliberately.

Years ago, an advertising man claimed that it was necessary to discover the 'Unique Selling Point' (the USP) of your product and push that in your advertising for all its worth. So all soap powders, detergents, instant coffees and the like tried to find one sales point which would distinguish them from their competitors. It is still good advice. Any advertiser who can find a theme which will separate his product or service from all the rest, and can exploit that difference in a sustained advertising programme, is bound to attract the attention of potential customers.

The important thing is not to clutter the message. When you consider the thousands of advertisements which fight for our attention every day, it is not difficult to appreciate the importance of a clear and simple message. Of course, we cannot all be creative geniuses who think up memorable slogans at the drop of a hat. But it is possible to make a believable statement in plain and simple language which most people will understand. Better this than a 'clever' statement which may confuse and be quickly forgotten.

What the advertiser wants above all else is for the customer to remember his name. Advertising can never replace personal selling - it is a complement to it. The sales message in most advertisements must be closed by a personal sales presentation, a sale over a counter, or even an order politely taken over the telephone. The advertisement is a sales aid and should, above all else, make the advertiser's name memorable. And if you have any difficulty remembering if it was Cinzano or Martini that Leonard Rossiter threw over Joan Collins, you will understand why.

SUMMARY

▍ Advertising on its own rarely sells products.

▍ Advertising is part of the marketing mix and complements or supports other marketing activities.

▍ Advertising creates awareness, conveys information, changes attitudes and reminds customers of the product or service.

▍ Advertising achieves the best results when working to clearly-defined, achievable objectives.

▍ Opportunities for advertising exist in the broadcast media, printed publications, indoor and outdoor posters and on many novelty items.

▍ Where possible the advertiser should find a theme which separates his products from his competitors, and promote this through a sustained advertising programme.

▍ The advertising message should be plain and simple, clear and uncluttered.

▍ What the advertiser wants above all else is for the customer to remember his name.

10 Direct Marketing

Direct marketing is different from most other marketing activities. Although sometimes used to complement or supplement other selling techniques, direct marketing should be able to stand alone. Its objective is to obtain a response, and sometimes to go through the complete sales message - attracting attention, arousing interest, creating desire and stimulating the customer into action, to buy the product or service on offer.

Growth in direct marketing in recent years has been considerable, and may continue for some time to come. Direct response advertising in printed media has always been with us, but direct response to television advertising is a comparatively recent phenomenon. Predictions for the future suggest that catalogue shopping via the television sets in our homes will add further impetus to direct response advertising, allowing the customer to receive and respond to the sales message, pay by credit card and take delivery without ever leaving his home.

Direct mail, once the Cinderella of the advertising profession, has increased in importance in recent years. With costs increasing all the time, and advertisers anxious to reduce wastage, the importance of sales targeting has spurred many to look more closely at a method of advertising to just those potential customers likely to be interested in the product for sale. Unfortunately, direct mail has also been used for blanket coverage, where those not interested in the sales message have reacted by calling it 'junk mail', a label which has stuck. With so many mailing lists on offer, there is no reason why this should be so. Any sales message which arouses interest and concern in the recipient could never be called 'junk', whether it is promoting sales of encyclopedias to students or inviting contributions for famine relief in Africa.

The List

One of the secrets of success in direct mail advertising is finding the right list. Today, hundreds of lists are available - from Active And Speculative Investors (624,702 of these) to Labour Saving Appliance Buyers (1,249,100), and from Vacuum Cleaner Repairers (500) to Tool Manufacturers And Suppliers (758). Agencies exist to provide these lists on paper and gummed labels, computer discs and tape. They may be sorted in many ways favourable to obtaining large discounts on postage, and may be personally addressed to 'The Managing Director', 'The Sales Director' and others. Duplicate lists may be provided for follow-up mailings and, sometimes, print-outs may be obtained, for a small additional charge, which provide telephone numbers for telephone sales follow-up.

Magazines sometimes sell their lists, and a direct mail shot can be an effective way of following up a regular schedule of display advertising.

It is important to remember that most lists are purchased for one-off use only. They will include a number of 'seeds' - names and addresses coded so that the list owners will know if a list has been used without permission and without payment. It is wise to check the usage restrictions when purchasing a list from owner or agent.

The Message

Having purchased the list, it is then necessary to compose a sales letter. For some advertisers, writing, especially within the disciplined structure of a sales letter, is extremely difficult.

The important thing to remember is that a sales letter is like a personal salesman. And some of the rules that apply to the salesman need also apply to the sales letter. For example:

▌ they both need to make a good impression at first sight
▌ their sales message should be expressed in terms the customer will understand

- the products or services they offer should respond to a specific customer need, and
- the benefits they have to sell should be clearly explained

There are ten things you should remember when writing and distributing a sales letter.

1 Think of a customer need you can satisfy.
All marketing begins with the identification of a customer need. Think of what you do well and who will benefit from it.

2 Begin your letter with some understanding of this need.
Let your prospective customer know that you understand his problem.

3 Explain simply and clearly how you can help.
Having identified the problem, show that you know how to resolve it.

4 Do not make any statement which is untrue.
Once found out, you will never be able to re-establish credibility with your customer.

5 Do not make claims you cannot justify.
It is pointless stating that you can perform certain tasks you are not qualified to undertake.

6 Remember that you will initially be judged on the quality of your presentation.
First impressions are important. Your sales letter should help you look professional and efficient.

7 Have your letter printed or copied on to good quality letterheadings.
You would want your salesman to look his best when first meeting a customer - so should your sales letter.

8 **Always use the Guild logo on your stationery.**
The Guild logo will add prestige to your sales letter. Where appropriate, mention your Guild membership in your letter.

9 **Sign each letter personally, if possible.**
This is only practical for small mailings. For larger distribution, have your signature printed on your letter.

10 **Ensure that your letters are delivered by a reliable agent.**
If delivered by hand, make sure that your letters actually do reach your prospective customers.

Examples of six specimen sales letters written for Guild members follow. Some Guild members may wish to use these in whole or in part to promote their skills.

▌ Other Direct Response Advertising

Whenever you attempt to obtain a direct response from an advertisement, leaflet or reply card, you are involved in direct response advertising. This may also include inserts and product cards.

More and more publications are now accepting inserts as publishers attempt to compete with the growth of direct mail. Although advertisers are sometimes concerned at high wastage levels, especially where some readers are seen shaking the inserts out of a magazine recently purchased, the fact remains that higher response rates are usually recorded for inserts than display advertising on a cost-per-response basis.

Product cards are packs of cards printed with a sales message on one side and a postage-paid return address on the other. Printing costs are absorbed in the individual card rate, and packs are distributed by magazines to their own mailing lists. They are usually confined to business-to-business advertising, and can be very cost-effective.

John Smith (Plumbing) Ltd
57 Bromfield Road
South Endean
Wessex
BX1 3RU

Dear Sir or Madam

My name is John Smith. I am a domestic plumber and a member of the Guild of Master Craftsmen. I work hard, and provide quality workmanship and prompt service at competitive prices. Few jobs are too large, none are too small, from the installation of complete central heating systems to fitting a new tap washer.

Perhaps you have a domestic plumbing problem which requires attention right now. If so, why not give me a call? You will be under no obligation, and an estimate will be provided for your approval before work commences.

On the other hand, you may be thinking of plumbing work in the weeks or months ahead. In that case it would probably make sense to keep this letter handy for future reference. In fact, why not do that anyway? **You never know when you might need the services of a good, economical, reliable plumber.**

I hope that I may have the opportunity of working for you.

Yours sincerely

(Signature)

John Smith
Proprietor

Jack Black (Electricians) Ltd
23 Coronation Road
Littlechester
North Cornwall
RZ3 2LJ

Dear Sir or Madam

It's a funny thing about electricity. We are so used to it in our homes we rarely give it a second thought - until it goes wrong! Just imagine if your power was cut off tonight: no television, no washing machine, perhaps no cooking and, increasingly often, no heating. Electricity, it seems, is always there, at the flick of a switch - until it goes wrong!

How long is it since your electric wiring was checked? Has it ever been checked? I am asking these questions because, if you do not know the answers, you may be interested in a special offer I am making to home owners in your area.

> **For just £x I will check the wiring in every room of a three or four-bedroomed house. I will express a professional opinion as to its quality and safety. If it is all right, I will say so. If not, I will suggest remedial action and provide an estimate for the repair.**

Please give me a call on (0937) 22734. I will be very happy to arrange an appointment to visit you at your convenience.

Yours sincerely

(Signature)

Jack Black
Proprietor

PS There is absolutely no obligation on your part to accept my estimate and you are, of course, free to obtain other opinions and estimates from anyone you choose.

George Green (Builders) Ltd
97 Lower Road
Westhampton
West Suffolk
KX10 3RG

Dear Sir or Madam

Have you heard about the local builder who takes on big and small jobs, works consistently to a high standard, keeps you informed of the costs as the work proceeds and leaves the site clean and tidy when he is finished? George Green is such a builder.

It does not matter what job you have in mind: building a fence or a wall, erecting a garage or conservatory, constructing a large or small extension, we are here to help. Just give me a call at your convenience; estimates and advice are offered FREE.

We are members of the Guild of Master Craftsmen and can provide recommendations and references on request. To us, quality is a standard, not just an aspiration.

Please feel free to call on us at any time. And if you do not have need of our services right now, please keep this letter in a safe place so that you will know how to contact us when the need arises. We are here to help.

Yours faithfully

(Signature)

George Green
Proprietor

Henry Doe (Building) Ltd
62 West Street
Sutton Bridge
South Merseyside
PQ1 7LF

Dear Sir or Madam

Your home is a major investment. When you consider the amount of money required to purchase, maintain and run even a modest house, flat or maisonette, it is no wonder home owners think twice when employing tradesmen to work for them. Exactly where do you look to find a reputable builder when planning improvements to your home?

Henry Doe (Building) has been working in this area for a number of years. Other homeowners close to you have employed us and are pleased with the quality of our work. In fact, it was through their recommendation that we were offered membership in the Guild of Master Craftsmen. We can show you examples of the work we have done to merit this award.

So if you are planning an improvement to your home - however large, however small - we would be pleased to be considered for the work. Our estimates are free; care and consideration for your requirements are part of our standard package.

Of course it is not every week that you need the services of a builder. We would therefore respectfully suggest that you make a note of our name and telephone number for future consideration. Then, when you have need of a quality builder to work on your home, please give me a call. I look forward to hearing from you.

Yours faithfully

(Signature)

Henry Doe
Proprietor

Barry Brown (Electrical) Ltd
27 Willenden Road
Haffenden Corner
East Surrey
KF21 3EG

Dear Sir or Madam

Have you ever wondered why, when you buy a new electrical appliance, there is never a free socket where you need one? And, no matter how new the house, there are never enough sockets in some rooms, and more than you will ever need in others? There ought to be a name for it - electrical aggravation, or something like that.

Never mind, a cure for electrical aggravation is at hand. It's called the Barry Brown (Electrical) service. Just give me a call and I will inspect your house with you, helping you decide what new sockets are needed and where; whether your current wiring is adequate and safe (now and for your future requirements); and quoting you a price for new sockets and any supplementary work that may be required. Needless to say, any estimates and advice are provided free of charge, and you will be under no obligation to accept either.

I am a fully-qualified electrician with many years' experience behind me. Such is the quality of my work that a number of my customers recommended me for membership in the Guild of Master Craftsmen. I feel certain that you will be equally satisfied with any work I may do for you.

So, if you are fed up with extension cords where sockets should be; are concerned that the wiring in your house has not been checked for some time; and would like to discuss your power requirements for the future as well as today, please give me a call. I will be pleased to hear from you.

Yours faithfully

(Signature)

Barry Brown
Proprietor

Brian Williams (Plumbers) Ltd
2 Westway Rise
Manton Wick
North Hertfordshire
WG3 7HR

Dear Sir or Madam

There is no doubt about it, when something goes wrong with the plumbing in your home, you cannot usually wait around too long for service. Blocked drains remain blocked, and burst pipes will continue to leak until they are repaired. But where do you go to find a plumber when you need one? That is where we can help.

We have worked in this area for many years - quite probably for one of your neighbours, at one time or another. The quality of our work is well known. As a matter of fact, a number of our customers supplied references to the Guild of Master Craftsmen to support our application for membership.

If you have need for the services of a good plumber, we would like to hear from you. If not, at this time, perhaps you would like to make a note of our telephone number - (0773) 34921 - and place it where you know you can find it in an emergency. When called upon, we will do everything possible to respond as quickly as possible to your needs.

Yours faithfully

(Signature)

Brian Williams
Proprietor

SUMMARY

▌ Direct marketing is concerned with obtaining a response directly from the coupon, leaflet or reply card provided.

▌ Direct response advertising on television will be a major growth area in the near future.

▌ Direct mail, accurately targeted, can never be described as 'junk mail'.

▌ One of the secrets of direct mail advertising is finding the right list.

▌ A sales letter is like a personal salesman, and similar rules apply to both.

▌ There are ten things for Guild members to remember when writing and distributing a sales letter.

▌ Inserts in publications usually produce a lower cost per response than display advertisements.

▌ Product cards are an effective means of advertising business-to-business.

11 Public Relations

Whether we realise it or not, we all have an image. Sometimes it is a little off-putting when we come face-to-face with that image, seeing ourselves as others see us.

It is no exaggeration to say that image is even more important than reality. If others see us as serious-minded, they react to us as though we are serious-minded despite the fact that we believe we are happy-go-lucky and humorous.

Companies, too, have images, and, as most senior executives understand, it is crucially important that this public face coincides with the image of the company they want to project. For example, it would be very bad today for any company to seem unconcerned about 'green' issues. If, as seems likely, consumers generally become more conscious of environmental issues, they may decide to reduce purchases from companies considered wasteful of scarce natural resources.

One company in Surrey which unintentionally and inadvertently discharged industrial waste into a nearby river, killing off a few dozen frogs, actually went so far as to import other frogs to replace them - and to make an announcement to that effect in the local newspaper.

This latter part of the exercise, making the announcement in the local newspaper, is what most people think of as public relations. In truth, public relations goes much further than this. Its concern should be the formulation of policy. In the example above, that would be the decision to replace the frogs in the first place. To work properly, public relations should never be a by-product of a company's activities - it should be the reason for many of them.

▊ Media Relations

What most people consider public relations is, in fact, media relations: a strategy to obtain favourable references to the company and its products in media read and observed by the company's publics, e.g.customers, suppliers, investors etc.

The reasons for attempting such an exercise are twofold. In the first place, if successful, it is a means of obtaining free advertising. Secondly, editorial space is a better salesman than an advertisement. It is the difference between you telling me how wonderful you are and someone else independently saying the same thing. Despite your well-deserved reputation for honesty, the latter is somewhat more believable.

▌Why Press Releases Fail

If these editorial references work favourably for the company or products mentioned, what is in it for the publications themselves? The answer should be news, information and items of interest for its readers. So many times companies seeking publicity seem to forget this - because their press release is relevant to them, they believe it should appeal to others. Often a moment's thought will show that this is not so, and that there is absolutely no reason why any publication should print their release.

One company in North America regularly sends a press release to newspapers around the world announcing the dates of their factory closedown for the summer holidays. It may justify a fee from the company's PR agency, but it is doubtful if any publication outside a 100-mile radius of the factory ever bothers to print it.

One evening newspaper in London regularly receives close on 1,000 press releases a week - only one or two of these are ever printed. The reasons for rejecting the majority are because they are:

▌ irrelevant
▌ inappropriate
▌ badly timed
▌ without news value
▌ poorly written

The average cost of writing and distributing a press release, including a photograph, is £4 each. On average 97% are wasted. This means that a successful press release costs around £135, still cost-effective in most media, but no justification for companies wasting time and money writing and distributing irrelevant and inappropriate press releases.

▌Writing a Good Press Release

The first thing any good press release should do is attract attention. An editor faced with 1,000 press releases a week, expecting most of them to be inappropriate and irrelevant, will not waste a lot of time reading each one. If the release has not gained his or her attention in the first two or three sentences, he or she is unlikely to read on.

Press releases should not be long and laboured. Short, punchy sentences in tight paragraphs should be captured in no more than 250 words. In that space all the questions relating to who, what, why, when, where and how, should be answered.

To be successful, a press release should have:

▌ a headline which is interesting and attracts attention
▌ a first paragraph which contains the main points of the release in no more than 50 words
▌ body text which is relevant not repetitious, flowing and not flowery
▌ points which are easy to understand and unambiguous
▌ short rather than long, difficult-to-understand words
▌ words that relate to the picture, if one is included
▌ the name of the product
▌ the important features of the product
▌ believable content

Distributing a Press Release

There are some 10,000 media outlets for your press release, about half of which are trade, technical and professional. Covering all of them, even at £4 a time, would be costly and extremely wasteful. Commonsense dictates that only those newspapers, magazines, radio and television stations likely to have some interest in the subject matter of the release should receive it.

One of the best sources of names and addresses for all media outlets in the UK is a publication called BRAD, which is published monthly by Maclean Hunter. Individual copies are rather expensive to buy, but they may be seen in the Reference Section of most public libraries.

The press release itself should be double-spaced; preferably, but not necessarily, on a single sheet. A photograph should be included whenever possible, and sent in a protective envelope. The envelope should be addressed to the editor by name (correctly spelt), if possible, handwritten, but certainly not impersonally addressed to the editor on a computer label. Where considered particularly relevant to the publication in question, it may help to phone ahead advising that the release has been despatched, and to follow that with a later call to ensure that it has arrived safely.

The Guild of Master Craftsmen Ltd

Castle Place, 166 High Street, Lewes,
East Sussex BN7 1XU
Telephone: Lewes (0273) 478449
Fax: Lewes (0273) 478606

SAVINGS ON A MILLION!

When every company in the country is anxiously exploring new ways to save money, the Guild of Master Craftsmen has recently introduced a new scheme for its 30,000 members which is *guaranteed* to save at least 10% on most commercial insurance premiums.

The scheme is underwritten by one of the largest insurance companies in the country and has already attracted £1 million in premiums from Guild members.

The special discounted rate was agreed after it was shown that Guild members, as a group, work well above average whilst having a claims record which is well below average.

The Guild of Master Craftsmen, whose members are employed in more than 300 different trades, crafts and professions, now provides a wider range of benefits than almost any other trade association.

For further information contact The Secretary, The Guild of Master Craftsmen, 166 High Street, Lewes, East Sussex BN7 1XU. Telephone (0273) 478449

Company Limited by Guarantee · Registered Office: 27/31 Blandford Street, London W1
Registered No. 1228315 · VAT Reg. No. 242 1775 74
Secretary: A. E. Phillips · Assistant Secretary: J. E. Owen

SUMMARY

I Companies, like individuals, have an image. This is important to the way customers and suppliers react to them.

I Public relations should never be a by-product of a company's activities but an active agent in formulating company policy.

I Media relations exists to obtain favourable references to the company in media read and observed by the company's audience.

I If successful, media relations is a cheap method of advertising. It can also be more effective.

I Press releases should be relevant, appropriate, correctly timed, newsworthy and well-written.

I Most press releases are wasted because they do not attract attention in the first two or three sentences.

I Only media likely to be interested in the subject matter should receive a press release.

12 Professional Help

Businesses, especially when young, are often managed by men and women with a special talent in one specific management discipline. If the business is technical, it is likely to have a technical specialist as chief executive. If it is sales-based, it is probably led by someone who climbed the management ladder through sales management.

It is unwise and unrealistic to expect these business leaders to suddenly become financial wizards, corporate strategists or business consultants simply because they have decided to start a business in which they are technically competent. Obviously extra management skills are acquired over a period of time, as learning by doing and learning by mistakes is inevitable, but there are certain to be moments when expert professional help is desperately needed. Where exactly should a harassed executive look for marketing help and advice?

▌First Steps

As stated at the very beginning of this book, every organisation has objectives. They are not always openly stated, but they are there. Spending a little time formulating and quantifying these objectives is a necessary first step before any professional help should be considered. Perhaps you want to increase your sales by 10% in real terms over the next twelve months and you have a specific sum of money available to achieve it. If so, you should say so. Your goal may be unrealistic in terms of your advertising budget, but better to find this out at the beginning than vaguely stating that all you want is to 'get some more business'.

Designers and others are often accused of overcharging when they have assumed (in the absence of advice to the contrary) that there were no specific restrictions on the money to be spent, and have designed a Rolls-Royce when a Lada would have done.

Companies are right to worry about professional specialists who spend clients' money as though drawing from an inexhaustible well of gold. But the only sensible way to combat this is to express clear objectives which have to be achieved within a finite budget.

▌ Finding Help

There are formal bodies for most specialist skilled groups of professional advisers. The Guild has directories and can supply lists if needed. It may be that your business is eligible for government assistance, especially under the enterprise initiative of the Department of Trade and Industry - check to make sure.

Apart from these routes, you may find help from referral by others. Professional advisers rely on recommendations from satisfied customers in exactly the same way that you do.

Before meeting any professional adviser you should:
▌ produce a summary of what your business does
▌ produce a summary of your objectives
▌ produce your plans, insofar as they are defined
▌ produce a draft of your requirements

At the meeting you should ensure that:
▌ the adviser understands your business
▌ the adviser provides references of work in related businesses - ideally not competitors!
▌ the adviser provides a copy of his contractual terms and conditions

After the meeting the adviser should:
▌ provide a full explanation of the services he expects to supply, clearly setting out his understanding
▌ provide an estimate, a timetable and a payment schedule
▌ send a contract for your acceptance and signature

You may find it necessary to go through this process more than once. It is worthwhile, ensuring that you establish a link with a business you can work with.

Once you have entered into a contract it is important that the adviser presents his outline proposals at an early stage, including, where appropriate, drawings and rough work for your consideration. This should give you peace of mind, as you can see his or her thinking in action before too many costs are incurred.

▌Advertising Agencies

It is wrong to believe that all advertising agencies are only interested in major accounts who spend large sums of money. Many agencies are small themselves and are anxious to take on small, ambitious clients they can grow with. The services they offer may not all be in-house; freelancers are frequently employed to provide artwork, design and copywriting. At the very least, though, even the smallest agency should provide a

proposed advertising budget, outlining all the costs you are likely to incur in achieving your advertising objectives, for you to approve.

Advertising agencies should be able to explain how these objectives will be achieved, the creative approach they propose for the planned campaign, the reasons why certain newspapers and magazines have been selected and others rejected, what leaflets will be printed and how and to whom they will be distributed, and so on. It is up to the advertiser to question the decisions made and possibly provide his own suggestions, especially where trade and technical publications are proposed, as he may have considerable knowledge of these.

Design Studios

Sometimes companies prefer to go directly to the specialist and leave out the intermediary. Design studios are capable of interpreting a brief and providing designs for advertisements and printed literature. Once again, a maximum expenditure level should be established and clearly explained if shocks are to be avoided at invoicing stage.

Guild Sales and Marketing Services

Frequently Guild members are anxious to obtain wider-ranging marketing advice than simply advertising and design. Often the Guild is contacted for help, and this can be provided where the request is clearly made. It should be presented in writing with as much background information as possible. The nature of the problem should be identified, and solutions already attempted should be described. Only when all the known facts are given can a really practical and effective response be made.

Business Counselling

There are times where members have gone so far down the road that their whole business requires the close scrutiny of a number of experts. The Guild operates a Business Counselling Scheme for just this purpose. The member is encouraged to complete a comprehensive questionnaire which, for a small fee, is scrutinised by the Guild's experts in marketing, finance, sales, property, taxation and insurance. Sound advice is given and solutions proposed.

SUMMARY

▌ Business leaders do not always have all the management skills necessary to operate a successful business.

▌ Marketing specialists are sometimes required to provide professional help and advice.

▌ The best results are obtained when marketing objectives are identified and quantified prior to seeking professional help.

▌ Advertising agencies should provide a complete service, from preparing a budget and promoting a campaign to the creation of advertisements and their placement.

▌ Design studios are capable of interpreting a brief and providing designs for advertisements and printed literature.

▌ The Guild provides sales and marketing advice to its members on request.

▌ The Guild's comprehensive Business Counselling Scheme looks at marketing, finance, sales, property, taxation and insurance.

13 Trade Associations

In Chapter 7, when we discussed selling the product, we mentioned the importance of making the right first impression. Later, when considering public relations, we discussed the importance of a company's image and how it affects the way customers and prospects view the company and the products and services it sells. In this section we will suggest ways in which membership of the right trade association can support and enhance a company's marketing efforts and help promote the right image to customers and prospects.

▌ Endorsements

Celebrities, as we know, are often paid vast sums of money to promote or endorse particular products - the reason for this, of course, is that these endorsements work. We may claim to be sceptical about the claims made in these advertisements, but the fact remains that they really do work. Sometimes the endorsement is not a direct one. Products used in films and soap operas, clothing and equipment used and worn by sports stars, even the Royal Warrant on a bottle or jar -

these are all subtle endorsements which encourage consumers to buy certain products in preference to others. And when you stop to think about it, why not? The first products we buy, as young men and women, are invariably recommended by parents and friends. These recommendations encourage that element of trust which, as we said earlier, is so essential in making a successful sale; essential not only before the sale, but also afterwards. Not so long ago research showed that the majority of new car advertisements were read by those who had recently purchased that same car; consumers looking for confirmation that the purchase they had made was the right one. Any company wishing to increase its sales would be wise to consider any promotional aid which endorses its products both before and after the sale.

Joining the Guild of Master Craftsmen

When a company joins a trade association, it distinguishes itself from those who do not belong. Automatically a new dimension is added to the company's sales message - it is like being told that a certain individual you recently met belongs to a trade union, supports a particular football club, or attends a certain university. This new knowledge may well change your perception of that individual, hopefully for the better, sometimes the reverse. That is why the decision to join one trade association in preference to another is so important for the future of your company and its development. If you are a widget manufacturer, membership of the Association of Widget Manufacturers will inform potential customers of what you do; unfortunately, though, it will not tell them how well you do it. This is where the Guild of Master Craftsmen comes in.

Customer Satisfaction

The Guild is different from most other trade associations for two distinct reasons. In the first place, before membership is approved, the Guild always insists upon receiving recommendations from recently satisfied customers. Think about this for a moment from a potential customer's point of view. To a new customer, this is very much like receiving an endorsement from a neighbour or friend, and is a very important point which all Guild members should include in every single sales presentation. Secondly, the Guild operates a recognised complaints procedure where any dispute between Guild member and customer is objectively and resolutely pursued until both sides are totally satisfied with the proposed solution. This objective approach is the customer's guarantee that his interests are taken into consideration, and this in turn enhances the confidence which the customer needs before deciding where to place his order. The Guild was established to promote those companies and individuals who take pride in what they do and act with honesty and integrity when dealing with customers. One of the published aims of the Guild is 'to protect the public by instilling among members a greater sense of responsibility, making members aware of the national importance of the services they render...and by encouraging members always to strive for excellence'. In placing customer satisfaction so firmly in the forefront of its objectives, the Guild believes it is assisting its members in the marketing of the products and services they sell.

▌Promotional Material

There is an old adage in the advertising business that says: 'You can't sell if you don't tell!' This is especially true in the use members make of the Guild logo. A whole range of promotional material featuring the Guild logo is available to members, helping them with the initial sales contact, where an introductory letter may be accompanied by an identity/compliments slip listing the aims and objectives of the Guild, right through to aftersales reassurance,

when the invoice arrives in an envelope overprinted with the Guild logo. In between, the member can reinforce the message of quality inherent in Guild membership with many other items, from ties and brooches to overall and blazer badges and from window and product stickers to van signs and contract boards.

The list of Guild promotional items is constantly being increased. This is because the Guild does everything possible to encourage members to display the logo at every available opportunity. The reputation of the Guild in the marketplace is enhanced every time a craftsman displays the logo - in the same way, members benefit every time the Guild's reputation is enhanced.

▌*Businessmatters*

Throughout this manual we have stressed the importance of advertising and promotion, as it is a vital part of every company's marketing mix. To assist members further, the Guild

encourages them to advertise in Guild
publications at very favourable rates;
offering generous discounts on display
advertising, and making a small,
nominal charge for typesetting when
taking classified advertising.
Businessmatters, with a readership in
excess of 100,000, is a wonderful
opportunity for members to offer
discounts to other members on the
goods and services they supply. More
than 1,000 members regularly
advertise to other members through
the pages of *Businessmatters*.

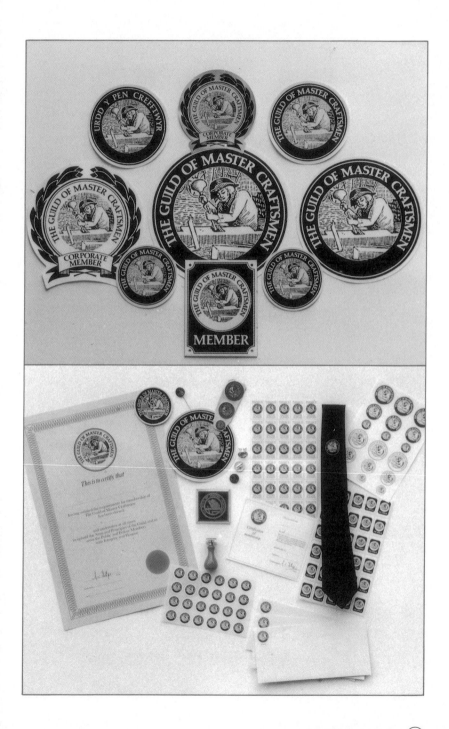

SUMMARY

▌ Guild membership supports and enhances a company's own marketing efforts.

▌ Recommendations from other satisfied customers encourage trust and increase the opportunities to sell.

▌ Aftersales reassurance confirms the decision made by the customer to purchase a particular product or service.

▌ Membership in a trade association, which emphasises the quality of its members' work, is reassuring to potential customers.

▌ Marketing seeks customer satisfaction: customer satisfaction is in the forefront of the Guild's aims and objectives.

▌ Guild promotional material allows members to exploit Guild membership at every possible opportunity.

▌ The Guild encourages all members to advertise in its publications at generously discounted rates.

14 The Marketing Plan

As should be apparent from the previous pages, marketing is more than a solitary management discipline. It interacts with every other aspect of the business and, in a truly marketing-oriented company, it is the cement which binds together all the company's resources in a totally integrated system. Because senior management is responsible for developing and running the company as a total entity - one which satisfies customers' needs at a profit - a marketing-oriented company is only possible with full encouragement and support from the top.

This means that the corporate strategy has to be right to begin with. For example, it may be sufficient to remain competitive in order to retain market share, but if the product is nearing the end of its lifecycle, an innovative rather than a competitive strategy may be required. That is why a marketing plan should follow clearly defined corporate objectives.

▌ Preparing a Plan

Large companies with professionally trained marketing departments may produce marketing plans which are two or three inches thick and form a major part of an annually updated five-year corporate plan. A small company with two or three dozen employees may produce a document of just a few pages. But for both of them, large and small, if they have any idea of where they want to be at the end of the year, they need to state their objectives and the method to be employed to achieve them clearly.

Once corporate objectives have been set, it is recommended that a detailed analysis of the organisation's strengths and weaknesses, and an assessment of the opportunities and threats likely to affect it, should follow. It may be that a weakness must be corrected or a threat dealt with before a particular objective can realistically be met. It could be that a certain company strength has opened the way to an opportunity not available before. Any of these could suggest a reappraisal of corporate objectives.

▌The Plan

There are many different ways of preparing a marketing plan. One of these is illustrated in the figure below. It is a simplified approach, designed for small to medium-sized companies, but one that can be made more detailed and elaborate as required.

A small, single-product company may well find the simplified grid structure adequate for its needs. The fact that the grid references apply to chapters and sub-headings in this book should make it simpler for them to do so. Larger companies will certainly require more detail, even if the basic system

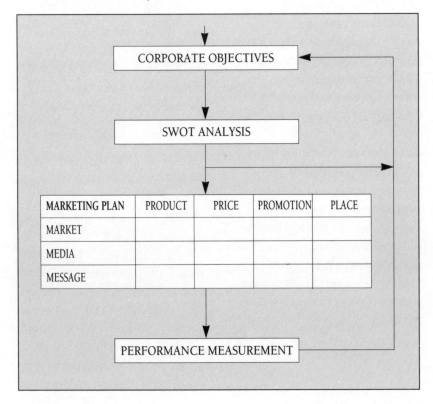

MARKETING PLAN	PRODUCT	PRICE	PROMOTION	PLACE
MARKET				
MEDIA				
MESSAGE				

(Flowchart: CORPORATE OBJECTIVES → SWOT ANALYSIS → MARKETING PLAN grid → PERFORMANCE MEASUREMENT)

set out here is to be followed. For example, the space occupied under 'Promotion' and 'Market' should list all the promotional opportunities for the product under consideration in one of its market segments. These might include newspapers, magazines, broadcast media, outdoor, point-of-sale, direct mail and public relations. The first entry, 'newspapers', might then be subdivided into national daily, national Sunday, local evening, weekly paid for, and weekly free newspapers. A further subdivision of national daily newspapers would include everything from the *Sun* to the *Financial Times*.

▌A Practical Example

Consider for a moment the practical construction of a very simple marketing plan. The example given is purely hypothetical and is intended to show how detail may begin to be added to the marketing grid in a first attempt to construct a marketing plan. The amount of detail finally included will depend upon many factors.

It is worth pointing out here that it is always tempting to continue collecting new facts as long as we are working with incomplete information. What we have to remember is that marketing is not an exact science. In addition, the collation of information can be an excuse for delaying implementation or an unwillingness to face up to the resulting success or failure of the plan. The rule to remember is that information is no longer valuable when its cost exceeds the savings it might bring.

Imagine, then, a manufacturer of frisbees - those small, plastic flying saucers which are thrown from one person to another. In our hypothetical example we will assume that the manufacturer has recently produced a new and different version of this familiar product. For the purposes of our marketing plan we may also assume that he is looking for large volume sales to a mass market. To sell in quantity he knows that his new product must sell for less than £5.

He will begin his marketing plan in the top row of the marketing grid, working his way across before proceeding to the next level. In the first square of the marketing grid, under 'Product' and 'Market', he will insert 'frisbees' and 'mass market'. The latter, in other examples, could easily be 'young men aged 18 to 25', 'housewives in Cumbria', or any other example of market segmentation - geographic, socio-economic or lifestyle. Under 'Price', our frisbee manufacturer will insert '£4.95'. Promotional opportunities could be display advertising, point-of-sale, radio and TV and direct mail. Distribution channels will include toyshops, garages and similar retail outlets plus, perhaps, direct-to-user fulfilment.

When he considers media opportunities, in the middle row, our manufacturer may believe that the product should be sold through certain newspapers and magazines with a strong youthful readership, certain independent radio and television stations and counter displays. In these media he might anticipate offering an introductory 10% discount off the recommended retail price. When considering the promotion of the new product in more detail, he might believe that only advertising in colour will illustrate the new product to its best advantage. This would restrict the media opportunities to magazine and point-of-sale, television advertising and colour advertisements in newspapers being beyond the limits of his advertising budget. Direct mail might also be excluded at this stage, simply because order fulfilment of a comparatively low-priced item would be too costly. This would restrict the distribution channels to toyshops, garages and similar retail outlets.

As far as the message section in the bottom row is concerned, although not looking for a definite and final creative approach at this time, one promising idea would seem to be a campaign built around the theme of 'Cheap Flights' - combining the physical appeal of the product with its low price. This then suggests a change from the 10% off introductory price offer to a competition offering cheap flights on scheduled airlines to glamorous locations around the world. It is possible that the campaign could be tied in with a particular scheduled airline who would offer fare concessions in exchange for the free promotion of their name. To make the most of this promotion, a specialist advertising agency might be engaged to develop a campaign which would help pull the product through the distribution channels.

▌Performance Measurement

In making these preliminary suggestions for marketing this hypothetical product, we have tried to show how a detailed marketing plan can develop through the systematic approach outlined in this book. Eventually a detailed plan will emerge with budgeted expenditure, targeted results and minimum performance levels. Sales territories, sales managers and representatives should all have expenditure levels and performance indices such as 'cost per sale', 'sales per month' and so on.

▌Feedback

Actual performance levels should eventually be fed back to see if adjustments may be necessary to the organisation's corporate plan. Unless there is an extreme variation from budget, any adjustment to corporate objectives is very unlikely. However, if sales are way below budget, or much above, or if the actual rather than the budgeted cost of sales casts doubt on the financial viability of the product, the sooner this information is relayed back, the quicker the organisation can adapt to these changed circumstances. Feedback from the marketplace is crucial in any marketing-oriented company.

SUMMARY

■ Marketing is more than a solitary management discipline.

■ Marketing interacts with every other aspect of the business.

■ New marketing initiatives receive encouragement and support from senior management in marketing-oriented companies.

■ Marketing plans must begin with clearly defined corporate objectives.

■ Corporate plans may have to be adjusted in line with the company's strengths, weaknesses, opportunities and threats.

■ The construction of a marketing plan should follow a systematic approach.

■ Levels of actual performance must be compared with performance indices in the marketing plan.

■ Constant and rapid feedback from the marketplace is necessary for a marketing-oriented company to accurately adjust its marketing plan in line with performance.

15 Your Silent Partner

The Guild of Master Craftsmen is a marketing-oriented organisation which knows and understands many of the marketing problems of its members. The Guild assists members with the marketing of their products and services in three different ways:

1 The Guild provides specific marketing advice to individual companies where full details of the problem are provided.
2 The Guild's logo provides reassurance to customers, thus helping members to make the sale.
3 The Guild provides a range of benefits which save money and time, thus permitting members to use these two valuable commodities in the preparation of their own marketing programme.

The Guild is every member's silent partner. A summary of the benefits currently available to members is listed below.

Professional Status and Public Recognition

Guild members are recognised for their expertise and integrity. Membership clearly separates them from the inept, the uncaring and the unscrupulous.

Extra Business Potential

Members of the public, businesses and institutions frequently contact the Guild hoping to find a craftsman with a particular skill in their area.

Debt Collection

A new scheme collects debts using a step-by-step procedure, from a formal solicitor's letter to an application for seizure of goods, with every stage priced separately.

Free Status Enquiries

Members contemplating long-term or exceptionally valuable contracts with other companies can obtain eight free reports annually and others at competitive costs to help them make their decisions.

Free Legal Advice

Members can receive expert professional assistance and advice on all business and personal legal difficulties.

Special Insurance Schemes

The Guild has negotiated a number of money-saving insurance schemes especially for its members which provide the right amount of cover at the lowest possible cost. They include:

▌ GROUP SICKNESS AND ACCIDENT

▌ PUBLIC AND EMPLOYERS' LIABILITY

▌ BUSINESS, COMMERCIAL TRADERS' AND SHOPKEEPERS' INSURANCE

▌ GOODS IN TRANSIT

▌ HOUSE, BUILDINGS AND CONTENTS

▌ PRIVATE, COMMERCIAL AND FLEET MOTOR INSURANCE

Guaranteed Discounts for Commercial Insurance

Any member spending in excess of £250 a year for commercial insurance is guaranteed a minimum 10% discount on renewal through this specially arranged Guild policy.

The Guild Logo

The Guild logo is a valuable trading asset. It enables potential customers to distinguish Guild members from others who could be unskilled and unqualified. The logo is featured on a wide range of promotional items.

Yellow Pages

Members may obtain listings in Guild corporate advertisements, enjoying the advantage of participation in a display advertisement at lineage rates and receiving public recognition for their skills.

Vehicle Advisory and Purchase Scheme

Independent and impartial advice with up-to-date price comparisons on all makes and models of vehicles, plus a guaranteed minimum of £500 off the manufacturer's current list price, is available to members.

Settlement of Disputes and Arbitration

In all disputes between members and their customers the Guild acts as an impartial third party, endeavouring to assist both sides in reaching an amicable settlement.

Discounted Private Health Plans

Western Provident Association offers a range of private health plan options at substantially reduced rates for Guild members. A 10% discount is available from BUPA.

Business Counselling
The Guild can offer sound ideas and suggestions to members for the improvement of their business from experts in marketing, finance, sales, property, taxation and insurance.

Sales and Marketing Services
Many members have received assistance from the Guild when confronted with specific sales and marketing problems.

Register of Members
A computerised register of members, classified by trade and geographical location, is maintained by the Guild in order to accurately respond to enquiries from members of the public, businesses and institutions.

Guild Publications
A generous 40% discount on all the Guild's best-selling magazines and books is available to members.

Reduced Advertising Rates
Members may place classified advertising in all Guild magazines for a nominal fee covering just the typesetting charges. Display advertising is discounted in *Businessmatters* and Guild magazines.

Businessmatters
The Guild publishes a regular magazine for members entitled *Businessmatters* which contains interesting and informative articles on matters closely affecting members and their businesses.

Member to Member Discounts
Many members offer generous discounts on goods and services to other members.

International Division
The Guild's International Division can put you in touch with sympathetic and allied craftsmen worldwide.

Contact With Other Crafts
Constant communication between members often leads to help and collaboration on specific projects.

NOTES

NOTES

NOTES

Other Titles Available From GMC Publications Ltd

Woodworking Plans and Projects
40 More Woodworking Plans and Projects
Woodworking Crafts Annual
Turning Miniatures in Wood   *John Sainsbury*
Woodcarving: A Complete Course   *Ron Butterfield*
Pleasure and Profit from Woodturning   *Reg Sherwin*
Making Unusual Miniatures   *Graham Spalding*
Furniture Projects for the Home   *Ernest Parrott*
Seat Weaving   *Ricky Holdstock*
Green Woodwork   *Mike Abbott*
The Incredible Router   *Jeremy Broun*
Woodturning: A Foundation Course   *Keith Rowley*
Upholstery: A Complete Course   *David James*
Making Shaker Furniture   *Barry Jackson*
Making Dolls' House Furniture   *Pat King*
Making Tudor Dolls' Houses   *Derek Rowbottom*
Heraldic Miniature Knights   *Peter Greenhill*
Electric Woodwork   *Jeremy Broun*
Furniture Projects   *Rod Wales*
Making Georgian Dolls' Houses   *Derek Rowbottom*
Woodworkers Career and Educational Source Book
Care and Repair 5th edition of the essential handbook
Directory of Members of the Guild of Master Craftsmen

GMC Publications regularly produces new books on a wide range of woodworking and craft subjects. Please write or phone for the latest information. All these books may be ordered by post from the publishers at 166 High Street, Lewes, East Sussex BN7 1XU, telephone (0273) 477374. Credit card orders are accepted.